DATE DUE

D1171103

LOCUST MIGRATION

BY L. E. CARMICHAEL

The Child's World

Published by The Child's World®
1980 Lookout Drive • Mankato, MN 56003-1705
800-599-READ • www.childsworld.com

ACKNOWLEDGMENTS
The Child's World®: Mary Berendes, Publishing Director
Content Consultant: Dr. Tanya Dewey,
    University of Michigan Museum of Zoology
The Design Lab: Design and production
Red Line Editorial: Editorial direction

PHOTO CREDITS
Rewat Wannasuk/Dreamstime, cover (top), 1, back cover; Eva-christiane
Wilm/Dreamstime, cover (bottom), 2-3, 29; Jinfeng Zhang/Dreamstime,
4-5; The Design Lab, 7; Leigh Diprose/Dreamstime, 8; Oliver Hoffmann/
Dreamstime, 10-11; Shih-hao Liao/Dreamstime, 12-13; Dreamstime,
14-15; Eric Isselée/Dreamstime, 15 (inset); Anton Ferreira/iStockphoto,
16; Mirosław Kijewski/iStockphoto, 18; Ruvan Boshoff/iStockphoto, 19;
Thaddeus Robertson/iStockphoto, 20-21; Paul Roux/iStockphoto, 22-23;
Julie Harris/iStockphoto, 24-25; Mykyta Starychenko/Dreamstime, 26-27

Design elements: Rewat Wannasuk/Dreamstime

ISBN 9781609736231
LCCN 2011940066

Printed in the United States of America

ABOUT THE AUTHOR: Lindsey E. Carmichael earned a PhD for studying the migration of wolves and arctic foxes in Canada's North. Now she writes nonfiction for children and contributes to the science blog, Sci/Why. Lindsey lives in Nova Scotia. She loves all of Laura Ingalls Wilder's books, including the one with the locusts.

TABLE OF CONTENTS

*Locusts are a kind of
short-horned grasshopper.*

LOCUSTS

There are thousands of types of grasshoppers in the world. Scientists separate them into two groups. Long-horned grasshoppers have long **antennae**. There are also many short-horned grasshoppers. They have shorter antennae and include locusts.

Huge groups of hungry locusts travel together in search of food. They may hop along the ground or fly. A group of locusts can be so big, it blocks out the sun. The insects' wings crackle like a giant forest fire. Locusts land on buildings, animals, and people. They cover every surface like a moving blanket. They eat every wild plant and crop in sight. Then they move on. They look for a new place to feed.

The locusts' lifetime journey is their migration. This is when an animal moves from one **habitat** to another. Migrations happen for many reasons. Some animals move to be in warmer weather where there is more food. There they can reproduce, or have their babies. And these migrations can be short distances, such as from a mountaintop to its valley. Or they can be long distances, like the locusts' journey.

MIGRATION MAP

Locusts live in hot, dry areas around the world. They only migrate when they cannot find enough food. Many years can go by in between locusts' migrations. Migrations can start at different times of year. They can start in different places. The paths locusts follow might be different every time. When locusts do not migrate, they live in **recession** areas. **Irruptions** happen when locusts migrate in large groups.

Desert locusts live in northern Africa, the Middle East, and parts of Asia. During migrations, they visit countries north, south, west, and east of these areas. Most often, desert locusts make loops around Africa and the Middle East. They usually follow the way the winds blow.

This map shows where desert locusts usually live and where they migrate to in large groups.

Irruption Area

Irruption Area

Recession Area

Recession Area

Recession Area

Irruption Area

Irruption Area

INDIAN

OCEAN

ATLANTIC

OCEAN

Recession Area

Irruption Area

THE WORD *LOCUST* MEANS "BURNT PLACE." IT COMES FROM THE WAY THE GROUND LOOKS AFTER LOCUSTS FINISH EATING.

A SPECIAL KIND OF GRASSHOPPER

Like all grasshoppers, locusts have six legs and bodies with three parts. Their eyes and antennae are on their heads. Their legs and wings attach to the thorax in the middle. Locust wings are longer than their abdomen. This is the last part of their bodies. Adult locusts are approximately 2 inches (5 cm) long.

There are different types of locusts. They include desert locusts, Australian plague locusts, and Rocky Mountain locusts. Different locusts are not really the same. They are more like cousins than like brothers or sisters. When they need to, millions of locusts can form a single group. The group migrates long distances in search of food.

Eyes and antennae are on a locust's head.

THE DESERT LOCUST

Desert locusts are found in 30 countries in northern Africa, the Middle East, and Asia. Locusts like to live in grasslands called the **savanna**. This habitat covers almost 10 million square miles (16 million sq km) of land.

Desert locusts are brown and green. They usually move around at night. Each locust avoids other locusts. They only come together when it is time to mate.

Male locusts sing to get females to mate with them. They do not sing with their voices. They rub one back leg against a back wing. This makes a chirping sound.

A desert locust uses its back legs to sing to its mate.

After mating, the female locust digs a hole in sandy soil. She pokes her abdomen into it. The female lays 60 to 90 eggs in one hole. Then she sprays the eggs with foam. The foam covers the eggs and keeps them safe. This creates an egg pod.

Each egg is the size of a grain of rice. Eggs need the right weather to **hatch**. Without rain, they will not hatch for weeks or even months. With too much rain, the eggs get destroyed. With just the right amount, eggs hatch in about two weeks.

HOPPERS

Locusts do not have wings when they hatch. They walk instead of flying. They also hop using strong back legs. Young locusts are called hoppers.

Rain falls in different places at different times in the savanna. Hoppers only hatch where it has rained. That is also where plants grow. Like adult locusts, hoppers have strong jaws. They can chew plants. Each hopper eats its own weight in food every day. The hoppers come out at night to eat.

Hoppers do not
have wings.

Green grass grows in the savanna after it rains.

Green patches grow in the savanna when it rains. These patches are like islands. Desert surrounds the islands. As hoppers eat plants, their islands shrink. Hoppers live closer together. They fight for the food that is left.

Then a very strange thing happens. The hoppers start bumping into each other. They see and smell the other hoppers around them. The hoppers start to change.

Hoppers want to be around other hoppers. They stop hiding from each other. They also let off a smell into the air. The smell tells other hoppers to join the group. The group is called a **band**. The hoppers change from **solitary** to **social** insects. This change takes just two to four hours.

Over time, the hoppers change in other ways, too. They change colors. They move during the day, not at night.

Hairs on the hoppers' back legs touch and then the insects know to change.

HOPPERS MAY
TRAVEL 15 MILES
(25 KM) FROM
THE PLACE WHERE
THEY HATCHED.

MOVING IN THE BAND

All the hoppers in a band move in the same direction. But hoppers do not follow a leader. The hoppers in the front of the band try to escape from hoppers in the back.

Hoppers bodies are filled with **nutrients**. That is why birds, **reptiles**, and people eat them. Hoppers also eat each other. This is called **cannibalism**.

Hoppers want to eat other hoppers. But they do not want to be eaten. Hoppers see group members coming up behind them. Then they move forward to get away. Soon, the entire band is moving in the same direction.

Hoppers eat other hoppers.

Hoppers shed their skin to grow.

SWARMING LOCUSTS

Hoppers **molt** to grow. This is when they shed their skin. Hoppers molt five times. It takes about 30 to 40 days. They do not grow wings until the last molt. Now they are adults.

Social hoppers become social adults. Social adults are different from solitary adults. They have bright colors. They move during the day. They also have longer wings. These long wings help them migrate through the air. These migrations are called irruptions.

MET FRANCISCO
LIBRARY

Social locusts travel in huge **swarms** when they migrate. There may be between 40 and 80 million insects in a swarm. One swarm of desert locusts may cover up to 400 square miles (644 sq km). It can take as long as six hours for the whole swarm to fly by.

All of the locusts fly in the same direction. Sometimes the swarm starts to separate. The locusts move back toward the center of the group. This keeps the swarm together.

Swarms fly in a tower shape. It can be up to 2.5 miles (4 km) high. The locusts at the top of the swarm pick its direction. They lead the group. They fly faster than the others. The leaders slow down if they cannot see the swarm. If there are plants below, the leaders land and begin to feed. Then the next highest locusts take the lead.

The back edge of the swarm passes by the locusts on the ground. Then the feeding locusts take off again. Some people say a swarm is like the tread on the wheels of a tank. When the front touches the ground, the back lifts up into the air.

Many locusts move together in a swarm.

CHOOSING A DIRECTION

Locusts can fly for many hours. They let the wind push them. The locusts save energy. Sometimes the wind blows locusts where they do not want to go. It can push them over lakes or oceans. If locusts get too tired, they might drop into the water and drown. Light that bounces off of water looks different than light on land. Locusts know each kind of light. If blown over water, the swarm flies against the wind. It moves until it reaches land again.

Sometimes swarms fly against the wind when there is no water around. That means locusts can choose their own direction. Scientists think locusts use light to find their way. Locusts can see where the sun is. The sun moves through the sky during the day. If a locust wanted to fly north, the sun would be on its right side in the morning. The sun would be on its left side in the afternoon. To use the sun, locusts have to be able to tell the difference between morning and afternoon.

Locusts can choose where to go.

GOING IN CIRCLES

The winds over Africa and Asia blow in different directions at different times of year. These winds push locusts in a loop. A swarm could end up back where it started in time. But the locusts that return would not be the same ones that left.

As they migrate, locusts land to eat and rest. The females in the swarm also lay eggs. Social females make a special foam to put on their egg pods. This foam tells the new hoppers to form bands. The hoppers will not live alone.

These new hoppers grow into social adults. These adults form a new swarm. Each swarm follows the migration.

Scientists think locusts migrate for two reasons. One is so the swarm can find enough food. The other is so females can lay their eggs in new places. That place may be better for the new hoppers. The original habitat may be full of food again when the locusts return.

Locusts land to eat, rest, and lay eggs.

THE SWARM'S END

A plague of desert locusts may visit many countries. A swarm can travel more than 186 miles (300 km) each day. Winds may carry locusts over 12 million square miles (30 million sq km) of land.

Locusts become solitary again after the swarm ends.

After enough time, even the biggest swarm dies out. **Predators** eat some locusts. Some are blown very far over water and die. Some swarms eat everything they can find. Then they starve to death.

The number of locusts gets smaller and smaller. With fewer locusts, there is less crowding. This makes the locusts change. They become solitary again. They start hiding from each other. They only come out at night. The locusts are now in recession. Becoming solitary takes time. This change happens over a few rounds of eggs.

IN 1988, A SWARM OF DESERT LOCUSTS WENT FROM WEST AFRICA TO THE CARIBBEAN. THE LOCUSTS FLEW 3,100 MILES (5,000 KM) IN JUST A FEW DAYS.

DEATH TO LOCUSTS

In one day, a swarm can eat enough food to feed 2,500 people for a year. Desert locusts visit many countries. They can eat the food that many people need to live. And desert locusts are just one type of locust. People have been fighting locusts for thousands of years.

Rocky Mountain locusts once swarmed across the prairies of North America. They ate the pioneers' crops. Many people had no food to eat.

Pioneers could not get rid of a Rocky Mountain locust swarm. They invented machines to kill hoppers instead. Some machines crushed hoppers into the ground. Other machines vacuumed them up.

The machine that worked best was the Robbins Hopperdozer. It had a blade that was coated with tar. Hoppers were scooped onto the blade. Then they stuck to the tar and died. Over 200 pounds (91 kg) of hoppers could be killed in one hour. That is more than 50,000 hoppers!

Locusts are killed with poisons today. It can take thousands of gallons of poison to stop one swarm.

The best way to kill a swarm is to stop it from forming. That means killing hoppers before they grow wings. Scientists use **satellites** to guess where bands of hoppers might form.

Crops are destroyed by swarming locusts.

The satellites take pictures of the savanna. They look for green patches where plants grow. People check those areas for locusts. If they find social hoppers, they spray them with poison.

Hopper bands live in smaller areas than swarms. Less poison is needed to kill them. These poisons kill many types of insects. They also hurt animals and people.

SAVE THE LOCUSTS

Laura Ingalls Wilder was an American pioneer and author. She wrote about locusts in her book *On the Banks of Plum Creek*. In 1875, a swarm of Rocky Mountain locusts destroyed her family's farm. Scientists believe that this swarm was the biggest there has ever been. They think it had 3.5 trillion insects. But by 1902, the Rocky Mountain locust was gone forever.

After many years, scientists think they know what happened. In the 1880s, pioneers moved to the Rocky Mountains. They built farms in the sandy soil of the mountain valleys. These areas were also the habitat of the solitary locusts. Farmers used plows in the soil. This hurt the eggs. Farmers watered their fields. The extra water destroyed locust eggs. Farmers also planted alfalfa. Scientists think locusts get sick after eating alfalfa. Farming may have destroyed the locusts' habitat. In just a few years, the locusts were gone.

Today, people spray poison on the habitat of desert locusts. It is possible that desert locusts will also go **extinct**. Many people believe this would be the best thing that could happen. Others do not agree. They feel we should keep the locusts safe. Locusts can be bad for crops. But they are a natural part of the world.

Locusts can harm crops, but they also help nature.

Locusts help nature in some ways. Locust bodies have lots of **protein** and healthy fats. They are an important food source for birds and animals. Some people also eat locusts. Locusts can be cooked fresh for dinner. They can be dried like raisins and used as snacks. Some people even dip locusts in chocolate and eat them as dessert.

Locusts also help plants. When locusts eat, they make space for new plants to grow. Locusts move nutrients over the land. They eat in one place. Then they move to another before they die.

Scientists think that prairies changed forever when the Rocky Mountain locust died out. They do not know what might happen if desert locusts disappear, too. Locust migration can be very bad for humans. But locust migration can help nature in many important ways.

TYPES OF MIGRATION

Different animals migrate for different reasons. Some move because of the climate. Some travel to find food or a mate. Here are the different types of animal migration:

Seasonal migration: This type of migration happens when the seasons change. Most animals migrate for this reason. Other types of migration, such as altitudinal and latitudinal, may also include seasonal migration.

Latitudinal migration: When animals travel north and south, it is called latitudinal migration. Doing so allows animals to change the climate where they live.

Altitudinal migration: This migration happens when animals move up and down mountains. In summer, animals can live higher on a mountain. During the cold winter, they move down to lower and warmer spots.

Reproductive migration: Sometimes animals move to have their babies. This migration may keep the babies safer when they are born. Or babies may need a certain habitat to live in after birth.

Nomadic migration: Animals may wander from place to place to find food in this type of migration.

Complete migration: This type of migration happens when animals are finished mating in an area. Then almost all of the animals leave the area. They may travel more than 15,000 miles (25,000 km) to spend winters in a warmer area.

Partial migration: When some, but not all, animals of one type move away from their mating area, it is partial migration. This is the most common type of migration.

Irruptive migration: This type of migration may happen one year, but not the next. It may include some or all of a type of animal. And the animal group may travel short or long distances.

> SOMETIMES ANIMALS NEVER COME BACK TO A PLACE WHERE THEY ONCE LIVED. THIS CAN HAPPEN WHEN HUMANS OR NATURE DESTROY THEIR HABITAT. FOOD, WATER, OR SHELTER MAY BECOME HARD TO FIND. OR A GROUP OF ANIMALS MAY BECOME TOO LARGE FOR AN AREA. THEN THEY MUST MOVE TO FIND FOOD.

GLOSSARY

antennae (an-TEN-ee): Antennae are thin feelers on an insect's head. Locusts' antennae are short.

band (BAND): A band is a group of locusts. Many locusts make a band.

cannibalism (KAN-uh-buhl-izm): Cannibalism is when an animal eats its own kind. Cannibalism happens between locusts.

extinct (ek-STINGKT): A type of animal is extinct if it has died out. The Rocky Mountain locust is extinct.

habitat (HAB-uh-tat): A habitat is a place that has the food, water, and shelter an animal needs to survive. Social locusts leave their habitat and move in swarms.

hatch (HACH): To hatch is to break out of an egg. With enough rain, locust eggs hatch.

irruptions (i-RUPT-shunz): Irruptions are when large groups of an animal migrate to another area. Irruptions do not happen at the same time every year.

molt (MOLT): To molt, an insect sheds old skin and grows new skin. Hoppers molt to become adult locusts.

nutrients (NOO-tree-untz): Nutrients are things that people, animals, and plants need to stay alive. Locust bodies have many nutrients.

predators (PRED-uh-turs): Predators are animals that hunt and eat other animals. Predators eat locusts for their fat and protein.

protein (PROH-teen): Protein is a nutrient found in all living plant and animal cells. Locusts' bodies contain protein.

recession (ri-SESH-uhn): A recession is a time when locusts are not migrating. In a recession, locusts live alone.

reptiles (REP-tilez): Reptiles are cold-blooded animals that lay eggs to have babies. Reptiles eat locusts.

satellites (SAT-uh-lites): Satellites are machines sent into space, which move with the earth's orbit. Scientists use satellites to see where locust swarms might form.

savanna (suh-VAN-uh): A savanna is a flat, grassy area with few or no trees. Locusts live in the savanna.

social (SO-shuhl): A social animal lives in a group, not alone. When locusts crowd together, they become social.

solitary (SOL-uh-ter-ee): A solitary animal lives alone, not in groups. Locusts can change from solitary to social insects.

swarms (SWORMZ): Swarms are large groups of insects that move together. Locust swarms can destroy entire crops.

FURTHER INFORMATION

Books

Kravetz, Jonathan. *Locusts*. New York: PowerKids Press, 2006.

Siwanowicz, Igor. *Animals Up Close: Zoom in on the World's Most Incredible Creatures*. London: Dorling Kindersley, 2009.

Wilder, Laura Ingalls. *On the Banks of Plum Creek*. New York: HarperCollins, 2004.

Web Sites

Visit our Web site for links about locust migration: *childsworld.com/links*

Note to Parents, Teachers, and Librarians: We routinely verify our Web links to make sure they are safe and active sites. So encourage your readers to check them out!

INDEX